MASTERING PHOTOSHOP 2025

A BEGINNER'S GUIDE TO UNLOCKING YOUR CREATIVE POTENTIAL

Amakashe Obed

Table of Contents

Chapter 1

Welcome to the World of Photoshop

What is Photoshop, and why should you learn it?

What is Photoshop?

Adobe Photoshop is a strong picture editing program that is extensively used by professionals and amateurs alike. It enables users to edit photographs, create digital art, and design graphics. Photoshop has established itself as the industry standard for image manipulation due to its comprehensive tool set and functionality.

Why should you learn Photoshop?

There are several reasons why you may desire to learn Photoshop.

• Enhance your photography using Photoshop's color adjustments, blemish removal, and creative effects.

• Use Photoshop to create visually attractive designs, including logos, posters, and social media graphics.

• **Increase Creativity**: Photoshop allows you experimentation with many creative techniques.

• Improve your employment prospects by learning Photoshop, which is required in many creative fields. Learning Photoshop might help you get a competitive advantage in the employment market.

• Learning Photoshop may provide personal enrichment by allowing for creative expression and the acquisition of new skills.

System requirements and installation for Adobe Photoshop 2025.

System Requirements

Adobe Photoshop 2025 requires the following system requirements for best performance and a pleasant user experience:

• **Operating system:**

Windows 10 (version 22H2) or Windows 11 (version 23H2), 64-bit only.

• **MacOS**: macOS 13 and 14 (14.4 or later).

• **Processor**: Intel 6th Generation or newer, or AMD equivalent with SSE4.2 capability.

• Requires 8 GB of RAM (16 GB+ recommended).

• Installation requires 15 GB of hard disk space, with extra space needed for online content downloads and temporary files during product use.

• **Display resolution:** 1440 x 900 (at 100% scaling factor).

• **Graphics**: Microsoft DirectX 12 compliant sound and display driver.

Installation

1.**Download**: Buy a Photoshop license from Adobe's official website or an approved store. Download the installation file.

2.To run the installer, double-click the downloaded file.

3.**Accept licensing Agreement**: Please read and accept the licensing agreement.

4.**Choose an Installation place:** To install Photoshop, choose the preferred place on your hard disk.

5.Click "Install" to start the installation procedure.

6.**Activate Photoshop**: Once installation is complete, you must activate your Photoshop license using your Adobe ID and password.

Additional notes:

• To download updates and use online services, a reliable internet connection is recommended.

• Keep your operating system and drivers up to date for best compatibility.

You may install and use Adobe Photoshop 2025 after satisfying these criteria and completing the installation procedures.

Navigating the Photoshop interface

Photoshop serves as your digital canvas. This is where you'll spend the most of your time dealing with photographs. Let us break down the important elements:

1. **Application Bar:**

• The horizontal menu bar at the top contains all necessary commands and choices, such as File, Edit, Image, Layer, and Select.

• The Options Bar, located below the Menu Bar, dynamically changes depending on the tool chosen. It offers specialized settings and choices for that instrument.

2. Document Window:

• The core display area for your picture or project. You may zoom in and out, pan around, and interact with the picture right here.

3. Tool Panel:

• The vertical panel on the left side offers tools for editing, painting, and choosing. Common tools include the Move Tool, Selection Tools (Marquee, Lasso, and Magic Wand), Brush Tool, Eraser Tool, and many more.

4. Panels:

• Customizable windows on the right side of workspace. They provide access to a variety of features and information:

The Layers Panel displays your image's layers and allows for easy organization, adjustment, and manipulation.

The Properties Panel shows properties for the chosen layer, tool, or object.

• **Color Panel:** Easily choose and control colors.

• The Brushes Panel allows you to customize brush parameters.

• The Character Panel controls text formatting and appearance.

• The Adjustments Panel allows you to modify brightness, contrast, and color balance.

5. Workspace Switcher:

• The icon in the upper right corner allows for rapid switching between predefined workspaces (e.g., Photography, Painting, Motion) or creating and saving custom workspaces.

Customize Your Workspace:

• Drag and dock panels to your desired location on the screen. You may also combine many panels to save space.

• Customize the Tools panel by adding/removing tools.

• Optimize your workflow by creating and saving specialized workspaces for various activities.

Understanding the layout and configuring the workspace to your preferences will allow you to use Photoshop more effectively and concentrate on your creative tasks.

Panels and Palettes: The Photoshop Toolbox

Panels and palettes are the key windows that surround Photoshop's document window. They provide you access to a variety of tools, options, and information that will be useful throughout the editing process.

Key Panels:

• The Layers Panel is considered the most crucial. It shows all of the layers of your picture and allows you to:

• **Organize layers:** Group related layers for better administration.

• Adjust layer parameters, including opacity and blending modes.

• Add layer effects, such as drop shadows, glows, and bevels.

• Create and update layer masks to determine which elements of a layer are visible.

• The Properties Panel provides properties for the currently chosen layer, tool, or object. Its contents vary dynamically depending on your decision.

• The Color Panel allows you to choose and control colors.

• Color swatches allow for easy storage and access of frequently used colors.

• Customize colors using the Color Picker, which supports RGB, HSB, and other color models.

• Color Libraries provide pre-made color palettes.

• The Brushes Panel adjusts the look and behavior of the Brush Tool.

• Choose from various brush tip shapes, sizes, and angles.

• **Brush Dynamics**: Adjust the brush's response to pen pressure, tilt, and other variables.

- **Brush Presets**: Create and store personalized brush sets.

- The Character Panel determines the look of text:

- Choose the font family, size, and style.

- Adjust character spacing and tracking.

- Adjust the spacing between lines of text.

- The Adjustments Panel allows for non-destructive adjustments to your image's color and tone.

- Adjust the overall brightness and contrast.

- **Levels**: Adjust the proportion of bright and dark tones.

- Create unique curves to change color and tone.

- Adjust the hue, saturation, and brightness of colors.

Customizing Panels:

- Panels may be docked on the sides or bottom of the workspace.

- **Grouping**: Combine many panels for better organizing.

- Panels may be tabbed to conserve space.

- Use the Window menu to show/hide panels.

Understanding and efficiently utilizing these panels will provide you with the skills necessary to produce amazing photographs in Photoshop.

Menus and Toolbars: How to Navigate Photoshop

Menus:

The menu bar, placed at the top of the Photoshop interface, allows access to a variety of commands and choices. Each menu item has a dropdown list of related commands.

• File commands include opening, saving, exporting, and printing files.

• **Edit**: Image editing commands include copying, pasting, altering, and filling.

• Adjust picture attributes such as size, resolution, and color mode using image commands.

• Commands to create, manage, and manipulate layers.

• Use the choose command to choose certain sections of a picture using different tools.

• Filter commands add different filters and effects to photos.

• **3D**: Photoshop commands for manipulating 3D objects and scenes.

• View commands include zooming, panning, and snapping.

• **Windows**: Panel and workspace management commands.

• Access help documents, tutorials, and support resources.

Toolbars:

The toolbar on the left side of the workspace provides a variety of picture editing and manipulation tools. These tools are divided into categories, and some have extra choices concealed behind them.

• Use Selection Tools to choose certain portions of a picture.

• **Crop Tool:** For cropping and straightening photos.

• The Spot Healing Brush Tool helps eliminate blemishes and flaws.

• The Brush Tool is used for painting, sketching, and retouching pictures.

• Use the Clone Stamp Tool to duplicate portions of an image.

• **Eraser Tool**: Removes sections of a picture.

• **Type Tool:** Add text to images.

• **Shape Tools:** For creating shapes and pathways.

• **3D Tools**: For creating and manipulating 3D objects.

By successfully utilizing the menus and toolbars, you may have access to a broad variety of capabilities and tools for picture editing.

Keyboard Shortcuts in Photoshop

Keyboard shortcuts are essential for effective and quick editing in Photoshop. Here are a few of the most important ones to get started:

General Navigation and Editing:

- To undo, use Ctrl+Z (Windows) or Cmd+Z (Mac).

- To redo, use Ctrl+Shift+Z (Windows) or Cmd+Shift+Z (Mac).

- To create a new document, use Ctrl+N (Windows) or Cmd+N (Mac).

- Open with Ctrl+O (Windows) or Cmd+O (Mac).

- To save, use Ctrl+S (Windows) or Cmd+S (Mac).

- To save, use Ctrl+Shift+S in Windows or Cmd+Shift+S on Mac.

- To close the document, use Ctrl+W (Windows) or Cmd+W (Mac).

- To zoom in, use Ctrl++ (Windows) or Cmd++ (Mac).

- To zoom out, use Ctrl+- (Windows) or Cmd+- (Mac).

- To fit an image to the screen, use Ctrl+0 on Windows or Cmd+0 on Mac.

- To see actual pixels, use Alt+Spacebar (Windows) or Ctrl+0 (Mac).

- **Hand Tool**: Spacebar.

- Toggle Full Screen Mode (F)

Layer Management:

- To add a new layer, use Ctrl+Shift+N (Windows) or Cmd+Shift+N (Mac).

- To duplicate layers, press Ctrl+J (Windows) or Cmd+J (Mac).

• **Delete Layer:** Delete Key.

• Toggle layer visibility using / (forward slash).

• To select all layers, use Ctrl+Alt+A (Windows) or Cmd+Option+A (Mac).

• Merge layers using Ctrl+E (Windows) or Cmd+E (Mac).

• Merge visible layers using Ctrl+Shift+E (Windows) or Cmd+Shift+E (Mac).

Selection tools:

• To select all, use Ctrl+A (Windows) or Cmd+A (Mac).

• To deselect, use Ctrl+D (Windows) or Cmd+D (Mac).

• To reselect, use Ctrl+Shift+D (Windows) or Cmd+Shift+D (Mac).

• To invert selection, use Ctrl+Shift+I (Windows) or Cmd+Shift+I (Mac).

Brush and Paint:

• Brush Tool (B)

• **Eraser Tool:** E

• **Clone Stamp Tool:** S

• **Eyedropper Tool:** I

• **Zoom Tool:** Z

• **Hand Tool:** H

Text tools:

• **Type tool:** T.

• **Bold Text:** Ctrl+B (Windows), Cmd+B (Mac)

• **Italic Text:** Ctrl+I (Windows), Cmd+I (Mac)

• To underline text, use Ctrl+U (Windows) or Cmd+U (Mac).

Colors & Swatches:

• Change foreground and background colors: X

• Default foreground/background color: D.

These are just a handful of the many keyboard shortcuts available in Photoshop. By learning and using these shortcuts, you may substantially speed up your process and increase efficiency.

Chapter 2

Working with Images

Open and Save Images in Photoshop

Opening Images

1.File > Open is the normal procedure. Go to the location of your picture file and select it.

2.**Bridge**: If you're using Adobe Bridge, you can browse and open photos right from the program.

3.**Drag & Drop:** Simply drag and drop the picture file from your computer's file system onto the Photoshop workspace.

Saving Images

• **Photoshop Document (.PSD):** Photoshop's native format. It retains all layers, changes, and other information, providing maximum flexibility for future alterations.

• JPEG (.JPG or.JPEG) is a widely used online and print format. It employs lossy compression, which means that some picture quality may be sacrificed to minimize file size.

The PNG (.PNG) format offers transparency and lossless compression, making it ideal for pictures with sharp edges or text.

• TIFF (.TIFF) is a high-quality format often used in professional printing. It can handle enormous file sizes and different color levels.

• **GIF (.GIF):** Enables animation and transparency. Typically used for tiny images and online banners.

Savings Tips:

• Use "Save As" to copy a picture with a new name or format while maintaining the original file.

• The Save for online (Legacy) feature optimizes photos for online usage by adjusting size, quality, and file format.

• Regularly save your work to prevent losing progress due to unexpected crashes.

Image Resolution and Quality.

• Resolution is measured in pixels per inch (PPI). Higher quality photographs are ideal for printing, whilst lower resolution images are better suited for online usage.

• **Quality**: The level of detail and color information in a picture. Higher-quality photos usually have bigger file sizes.

Understanding the various file formats and saving choices allows you to guarantee that your photographs are saved in the correct format for their intended usage.

File Formats and Compatibility in Photoshop

Understanding file formats is critical for ensuring that your photographs work with various apps and devices.

Here's an overview of several popular file types and their features.

Photoshop Document (PSD):

• Photoshop's native format preserves layers, changes, and other information.

• Perfect for working files, revising projects, and maintaining flexibility.

• **Compatibility**: Adobe Creative Suite is recommended, however alternative image editing tools may provide limited functionality.

JPEG (.JPG/.JPEG):

• Widely accepted format for online pictures, social networking, and digital photography.

• Lossy compression reduces file size by deleting picture data.

• Optimal for photos and graphics with smooth color gradients.

• Compatible with practically all picture viewers and applications.

PNG (.png):

• Supports transparency, making it ideal for photos with sharp edges, logos, or translucent backgrounds.

• Lossless compression ensures picture quality without data loss.

• Perfect for web graphics, logos, and text-based visuals.

• Compatible with most browsers, however older ones may have limited support for transparency.

TIF (.TIFF):

• High-quality format suitable for professional printing and preservation.

• Supports big file files and many color depths.

• **Optional lossless compression**: Save data with or without compression.

• Ideal for high-resolution photographs, printing, and archiving.

• Compatible with a wide range of professional image editing and printing applications.

Gif (.GIF):

• Enables animation and basic transparency.

• **Lossless compression:**

• Ideal for simple animations, minimal images, and online banners.

• **Compatibility**: Widely supported, but restricted color pallet (256).

Selecting the Right Format:

• Consider the image's intended use: online, print, or personal.

• Determine whether the picture requires high resolution and precise color reproduction.

• Determine if the picture requires further editing or may be utilized with translucent backgrounds.

Understanding the benefits and limits of various file formats allows you to choose the best one for your unique requirements while also ensuring compatibility across several platforms and apps.

Image Resolution and Quality in Photoshop.

Image Resolution

• picture resolution is the level of detail in a picture, measured in PPI or DPI.

• Higher resolution means more pixels crammed into a given space, resulting in sharper and clearer visuals.

• Common resolutions:

• 72 PPI is often suitable for online usage.

• High-quality printing requires a minimum of 300 PPI

Image Quality

• Image quality refers to an image's entire visual appearance, including sharpness, color correctness, and lack of artifacts.

• Factors affecting quality:

• Higher resolution often results in higher quality.

• TIFF and PNG are lossless file formats that retain more picture data than JPEG, which is a lossy format.

• Excessive compression might reduce picture quality.

• Improper editing may cause artifacts and reduce picture quality.

Resizing Images with Photoshop.

• Use the Image > Image Size dialog box to adjust an image's size (width and height).

• When resizing a picture, choose the appropriate resampling technique.

• The simplest approach, Nearest Neighbor, might result in significant abnormalities.

• Bilinear is a smoother technique, but may lose detail.

• **Bicubic**: Offers optimal results for most photos, but may be slower.

• Preserve Details (Enlargement Only): Enlarge photos with minimal artifacts.

Tips to Maintain Image Quality:

• Use high-resolution source photos wherever feasible.

• Repeatedly scaling a picture may reduce its quality.

• Select the suitable resampling technique for your requirements.

• Optimize picture quality by saving in lossless formats such as TIFF or PNG.

Understanding the link between resolution and quality allows you to make educated choices about how to resize and save photos in Photoshop for the best results.

Cropping images in Photoshop.

• Locate the Crop Tool () in the Tools panel.

• Create a crop box around your picture. Adjust the size and form of the crop box by dragging the handles.

• To place the crop box, drag it inside the picture.

• To rotate the crop box, drag outside one of its corner handles.

• Lock crop box aspect ratio to retain proportions (4:3, 16:9).

• To straighten slanted horizons or skewed lines, use the Straighten tool () in the Options box.

Tips for Effective Cropping:

• Use the Rule of Thirds to divide the picture into nine equal pieces, each with two horizontal and two vertical lines. Place significant items along these lines or at their crossings to create a more balanced design.

• Crop the picture to highlight the primary topic and eliminate distracting items.

• Select a backdrop that compliments the topic and improves the overall composition.

• Experiment with crop ratios and locations to get the best visual composition.

Straightening Images using Photoshop

• To use the Crop Tool, activate the Straighten tool () under the Crop Tool settings.

• To draw a straight line in a picture, click and drag it along a horizontal or vertical feature that should be straight (e.g., horizon, building edge).

• Photoshop will straighten your picture depending on the angle of the line you created.

Mastering cropping and straightening procedures can help you enhance the composition and visual appeal of your photographs.

Resizing Images with Photoshop.

Resizing photographs in Photoshop is a regular activity, whether you're preparing them for the web, printing, or another application. Here's a breakdown of the procedure:

1. **Accessing the Image Size Dialogue Box:**

• Navigate to Image > Image Size. This opens the Image Size dialog box.

2. **Key Features of the Image Size Dialog Box:**

• Enter the desired picture width and height in pixels.

• **Resolution**: Measured in pixels per inch (PPI).

• For online, 72 PPI is often adequate.

• For printing, 300 PPI is the threshold for high-quality results.

• **Constrain Proportions**: Maintains the image's original aspect ratio and prevents deformation.

• **Resample**: This option controls how Photoshop adds or removes pixels while scaling.

- The simplest approach, Nearest Neighbor, might result in apparent artifacts when expanding.

- Bilinear is a smoother technique, but may lose detail.

- Bicubic gives optimal results, particularly for picture enlargement.

- **Preserve Details (Enlargement Only):** Optimized for picture enlargement with minimal artifacts.

3. Resizing Process:

- To change the measurements, enter the required width and height or use the sliders.

- Select the suitable resampling technique for the picture and desired output.

- **Click OK:** Photoshop will resize the picture to your needs.

Tips on Resizing:

- To maintain the aspect ratio, tick the "Constrain Proportions" option to prevent picture distortion.

- Experiment with various resampling algorithms to get optimal results for your picture.

- **Consider file size:** Resizing may greatly impact file size. If you're dealing with online pictures, aim for a balance between image quality and file size.

- Preserve the original picture by saving a duplicate before shrinking it.

By following these methods and knowing the main ideas, you can properly resize photos in Photoshop to meet a variety of demands.

Chapter 3

Selection Tools

The Selection Tool Suite

The Marquee Tools in Photoshop are a collection of selection tools that enable you to make different shapes and sizes of selections inside your picture. They are crucial for isolating certain portions of a picture for editing, adding effects, or rearranging components.

Types of Marquee Tools:

• The Rectangular Marquee Tool creates rectangular or square selections.

• Use the Elliptical Marquee Tool to create elliptical or circular selections.

• The Single Row Marquee Tool selects a single row of pixels.

• The Single Column Marquee Tool selects a single column of pixels.

Using the Marquee Tool:

1.Select the required Marquee Tool from the Tools menu.

2.Create a selection:

• To make a selection, click and drag your cursor over the picture.

• **Holding Shift:** Limits the selection to a perfect square or circle.

• Holding Alt/Option creates a selection from center outward.

3.Refine your selection (optional):

• To soften the margins of the selection, apply a feathery border.

• Use the Refine Edge tool to increase selection precision.

• **Common Applications of Marquee Tools:**

• Isolate items in a picture to edit, move, or apply effects.

• To create backgrounds, select and delete an image's background.

• **Adjustments**: Apply color, filters, or effects to particular sections of a picture.

• To create composite photos, choose and chop out certain components from many photographs.

By learning the Marquee Tools, you will have more control over your picture editing process and be able to make more accurate choices.

Photoshop's Lasso Tools are a series of selection tools that allow you to make freehand selections around oddly shaped objects or regions in images. They provide flexibility when the hard forms of the Marquee Tools are not appropriate.

Types of Lasso Tools:

• The Lasso Tool provides basic freehand selecting capabilities. You drew a freehand outline of the intended region.

Tip: Use the Shift key to draw straight lines between locations.

• The Polygonal Lasso Tool connects straight lines to generate precise selections.

Tip: Click to establish anchor points, then link them. Double-click to finish the selection.

• The Magnetic Lasso Tool is useful for tracing complicated forms since it "snaps" to high contrast edges.

Tip: Adjust the "Frequency" and "Edge Contrast" settings in the Options box to customize the behavior.

Common Applications of Lasso Tools:

• Isolate objects with complicated shapes, such as hair, leaves, or clouds.

• Isolate certain sections of a picture for editing or effects by creating accurate masks.

• **Extracting elements**: Separate items from their backgrounds for reuse in other projects.

Tips for Using Lasso Tools:

• Zoom in to make exact choices.

• Use the Refine Edge tool to improve the accuracy and smoothness of your selection.

• The Lasso Tools need practice to master. Experiment with several ways to see what works best for you.

By utilizing the Lasso Tools correctly, you may make complicated and precise choices that were previously impossible to do.

The Magic Wand Tool in Photoshop is a strong selection tool that makes it easier to choose sections of a picture that have similar hue or tone.

How It Works:

• The Magic Wand tool chooses adjacent pixels with similar hue and tone when you click on a certain color in a picture.

• The "Tolerance" choice in the Options tab controls the tool's color selection range. A higher tolerance picks a broader range of colors, while a lower tolerance selects a smaller range.

Common uses:

• Easy to pick vast regions of solid color backdrops.

• Isolate items with unique color borders from their backgrounds.

• Quickly remove backgrounds from photographs to utilize in other projects.

• **Use Effects:** Add color tweaks, filters, and other effects to specific sections of a picture.

How to Use the Magic Wand Tool Effectively:

• Experiment with various tolerance settings to attain desired results.

• Select colors from all visible layers in your picture by using the "Sample All Layers" option.

• Use the Refine Edge tool to increase picture selection accuracy, particularly for intricate edges.

• For sophisticated choices, use the Magic Wand Tool with additional selection tools such as the Lasso or Pen.

Limitations:

• Images with slight color fluctuations or intricate borders may not perform well.

• Can occasionally choose undesired regions.

Understanding the Magic Wand Tool and its settings allows you to swiftly and effectively choose big sections of comparable hue within your photographs, so optimizing your workflow.

Quick Selection Tool

The rapid Selection Tool in Photoshop is a useful tool for producing rapid and efficient choices.

How It Works:

• The Quick Selection Tool examines color and edges to establish the object's limits, unlike the Magic Wand that just chooses by color.

• The tool widens the selection depending on color, texture, and edges as you "paint" over the desired region.

Key features:

• **Ease of Use:** Popular among Photoshop users because to its straightforward and user-friendly interface.

• Faster selection of complicated items than other tools.

• Seamlessly combines with the Refine Edge tool for enhanced accuracy.

Common uses:

• Quickly choose things with irregular forms, such as hair, fur, or leaves.

• Isolate items from their backgrounds for reuse in projects.

• Use masks to make effects or modifications to particular sections of a picture.

Tips for using the Quick Selection Tool:

• Use bracket keys ([and]) to easily modify brush size for greater control.

• Use the Refine Edge tool to get crisp edges.

• For sophisticated choices, use the Quick Selection Tool with additional tools such as the Lasso or Magic Wand.

Mastering the Quick Selection Tool allows you to greatly expedite your productivity and make professional-looking choices with no effort.

The choose Subject tool in Photoshop is a sophisticated AI-powered function that transforms how you choose items inside a picture.

How It Works:

• Select topic, powered by Adobe Sensei, intelligently analyzes images and determines the primary topic.

• **One-Click Selection:** Simply click to choose the image's main topic.

• High accuracy in distinguishing various topics, such as humans, animals, automobiles, and complicated objects.

Key Benefits:

• Improves speed and efficiency by reducing the time spent manually picking things.

• Accurate choices, even for difficult themes.

• **Versatile**: Suitable for many photos and themes.

How To Use:

• To choose a subject, go to the choose menu and click "Subject."

• Photoshop's One-Click Selection feature automatically selects the primary topic in a picture.

• Use the Refine Edge tool to improve selection for complicated objects or tough edges.

Limitations:

• Selection accuracy varies based on picture complexity and topic.

• Refine your choices using the Refine Edge tool for best results.

Overall:

The Select Subject tool revolutionizes picture editing in Photoshop. It greatly simplifies the selecting process, enabling you to concentrate on more creative activities. While it may not be ideal in all situations, it is a useful tool that may save you a lot of time and work.

The Refine Edge tool in Photoshop is a useful function for fine-tuning selections, particularly ones with complicated edges such as hair, fur, or detailed details. It greatly increases the precision and fluidity of your picks.

Accessing Refine Edge:

• To refine the edge after making an initial selection using any selection tool (Marquee, Lasso, Magic Wand, Quick Selection, or Select Subject), use the "Refine Edge" button in the Options Bar.

• To refine the edge, use the Select menu.

• Use the Select and Mask Workspace to refine your choices. You may get to it by selecting the "Select and Mask" button in the Options bar of any selection tool, or by navigating to Select > Select and Mask.

Key features of the Refine Edge Tool:

• Photoshop's Edge Detection feature analyzes images to find topic edges.

• **Radius**: Adjusts the breadth of the edge refining area.

• Smooths off rough edges.

• **Feather**: Softens selection edges with a gentle transition.

• **Contrast**: Adjusts the contrast between the topic and backdrop.

• **Shift Edge:** Repositions the selection's edge inward or outward.

• **Decontaminate Colors:** Removes color pollution from the selection's edges.

• **Output**: Specifies how the refined selection is applied (e.g., as a layer mask, new layer, or selection).

• Use View Mode to examine selections with multiple backdrop colors or overlays for a better visual representation.

Use Refine Edge Effectively:

1.**Make an Initial Selection**: Using any selection tool, build an initial selection centered on the topic.

2.Open the Refine Edge dialog box.

3.**Adjust options:** Experiment with different options to fine-tune your choices.

4.**Examine the Results**: Use the various view modes to examine the selection and make changes as necessary.

5.**Output the Selection**: Select how you wish to apply the refined selection (e.g., layer mask).

Tips for Refining Selections:

- **Zoom In**: Make exact modifications by focusing on certain regions.

- Use the Refine Edge Brush to refine regions.

- Experiment with settings to optimize your photograph.

Mastering the Refine Edge tool allows you to create very precise and professional-looking choices in Photoshop.

Chapter 4

Layers

Layers are the foundation of Photoshop

Layers in Photoshop are like stacks of translucent sheets. Each layer may include an image element, such as a picture, shape, text, or modification. This layered structure is essential for non-destructive editing in Photoshop.

Key concepts:

• **Non-Destructive Editing**: Layers allow for image adjustments without permanently affecting the original pixel data. This lets you explore and simply undo or adjust your changes later.

• Layers provide amazing versatility. You can do:

• Rearrange layers to determine which are visible on top.

• To control the visibility of each layer, modify its transparency.

• To apply layer styles, add effects like as drop shadows, glows, and bevels to each layer.

• To create sophisticated effects, use layer masks to hide or display certain layers.

• Organize layers into groups for effective management.

Types of Layers:

• **Image Layers:** Store pictures or photos.

• Text Layers include text components.

• Shape Layers include vector shapes.

• **Adjustment Layers**: Make non-destructive color and tone tweaks to the layers underneath.

The Layers Panel:

The Layers panel is the main interface for managing layers. It shows a list of all the layers in your document, as well as icons for layer visibility, blending modes, and other options.

Mastering Layers:

Understanding layers is essential for efficient and successful picture editing in Photoshop. Layers allow you to easily and precisely construct complex and complicated graphics.

Creating, duplicating, and deleting layers

Absolutely! Let's look at how to create, duplicate, and delete layers in Photoshop.

Creating Layers

• To create a new layer, just click the "Create a New Layer" button located at the bottom of the Layers panel. It resembles a square piece of paper.

• To create a layer, go to the "Layer" menu, pick "New," and then "Layer." A dialog box will appear where you may name and alter the layer's properties.

• **Keyboard shortcut:** Press Ctrl+Shift+N (Windows) or Cmd+Shift+N (Mac).

Duplicating layers

• To quickly duplicate a layer, use the keyboard shortcut Ctrl+J (Windows) or Cmd+J (Mac).

• To duplicate a layer, hold Alt (Windows) or Option (Mac) and drag it to the "Create a New Layer" icon at the bottom of the Layers panel.

• To duplicate a layer, use the Layer Menu and click "OK."

Deleting Layers

• To remove a layer, just drag it to the trash can icon at the bottom of the Layers panel.

• Keyboard shortcut: Select the layer and click the Delete key.

• To delete a layer, use the Layer Menu and choose Layer > Delete Layer.

Key Considerations

• **Layer Order**: The order of layers in the Layers panel decides which layers appear on top. Layers may be simply rearranged by clicking and dragging them into a new place.

• **Layer Visibility:** The eye symbol next to each layer in the Layers panel determines its visibility. To conceal or expose a layer, click on the eye symbol.

• Use descriptive layer names to maintain track of them, particularly in large projects.

Mastering these essential layer techniques will give you more control over your Photoshop work and open up new creative possibilities.

Layer Blending Modes: How They Interact

In Photoshop, layer blending modes control how a layer's colors interact with the colors of layers underneath it. By default, layers are set to "Normal" mode, which means they sit on top of the levels below. Photoshop, on the other hand, has a diverse set of blending settings that may achieve dramatic and imaginative results.

Understanding blending modes:

• Each blending mode uses a mathematical formula to mix the active layer's colors with those of the underlying layers.

• Common blending modes:

• **Multiply**: Darkens colors that overlap.

• **Screen**: Lightens colors that overlap.

• **Overlay**: Achieves a balance between Multiply and Screen based on the underlying color.

• **Soft Light**: Colors are subtly lightened or darkened, akin to a soft light.

• Hard light is more dramatic than soft light, resulting in greater contrast.

• To get a high-contrast appearance, remove the color of the base layer from the blend layer.

• Exclusion is similar to Difference but has a subtler impact.

• Color Dodge lightens the base layer's colors.

• Color Burn darkens the base layer's hues.

• **Using blending modes:**

• To alter a layer's blending mode, first select it.

• To pick a blending mode, click the dropdown menu next to "Normal" in the Layers panel.

• Experiment with various blending modes to observe how they alter your image's look.

Tips for Blending Modes:

• Experimentation is key, since there are no strict restrictions. Experiment with various mixing modes to get the results that suit you best.

• When utilizing blending modes, layer order is crucial for optimal results.

• Combine blending modes with layer masks for more control and versatility.

Understanding and exploiting layer blending modes allows you to generate a variety of creative effects in Photoshop, from subtle color modifications to stunning special effects.

Layer masks provide non-destructive control over layers

Layer masks are very powerful Photoshop tools that enable you to adjust the visibility of certain sections inside a layer while preserving the original pixel data.

How Layer Masks Work:

• **Black Hides, White Reveals**: A layer mask is a grayscale image that overlays your layer. Black portions on the mask conceal the corresponding layers, while white ones disclose them. Gray regions produce different levels of transparency.

• **Non-Destructive**: The mask does not modify the layer's pixels, allowing for easy editing and removal without impacting the original picture data.

Creating Layer Masks

• **From a selection**:

• Make a pick around the area to reveal.

• To add a layer mask, click the "Add Layer Mask" button at the bottom of the Layers panel (it appears as a rectangle with a circle).

• Photoshop creates a layer mask based on your selection, displaying the chosen region while obscuring the rest.

• To expose the full layer, use the "Add Layer Mask" option.

Editing Layer Masks:

• To obscure areas of a layer, use black paint on the layer mask.

• Use white paint on the layer mask to show certain layers.

• To achieve different levels of transparency, paint with gray on the layer mask.

• To invert the mask, use Ctrl+I (Windows) or Cmd+I (Mac) to show and hide regions.

Key Applications of Layer Masks:

• Isolate and clip off certain items in a picture.

• Seamlessly mix numerous photos together.

• Create special effects by adjusting certain portions of a photograph.

• Fine-tune edges of choices made with other tools.

Mastering layer masks will give you unequaled control over your photographs and open you a world of creative possibilities in Photoshop.

Layer Groups: Organize Your Photoshop Workflow

Layer groups function similarly to Photoshop folders. They help you organize your project by grouping relevant layers together, making it simpler to explore, edit, and manage your content.

Creating layer groups:

• Click the "Create a New Group" icon, which appears as a little folder at the bottom of the Layers panel.

• To group layers, first select them, then right-click and choose "Group Layers."

Add Layers to a Group

• To add layers to a group folder in the Layers panel, just drag and drop them.

Working With Layer Groups:

• To change the visibility of a group's layers, click the eye symbol next to the group folder.

• **Editing**: Apply tweaks, effects, or layer styles to a group to affect all layers inside it.

• **Nesting**: Create groups inside groups for a more ordered layer structure.

• To rename a group, double-click on its name in the Layers panel for greater clarity.

Advantages of Using Layer Groups:

• **Improved Organization**: Easier to identify and manage layers in complicated projects.

• **Improved efficiency:** Easily modify and apply effects to numerous layers at once.

• Improves workflow by organizing and managing projects.

By correctly employing layer groups, you may improve your Photoshop productivity and produce more complicated and structured projects.

Chapter 5

Retouching and Enhancements

Remove Blemishes and Imperfections in Photoshop

Photoshop has various strong tools to erase flaws and defects from your photographs, including:

1. Spot Healing Brush Tool:

• Ideal for removing tiny imperfections such as pimples, freckles, and dust spots.

How it works:

• **Content-Aware**: Removes blemishes by analyzing the surrounding area and blending perfectly.

• Simply click on the flaw and Photoshop will replace it with similar pixels.

2. Healing Brush Tool:

• Ideal for removing bigger defects or faults that demand precision.

• How it works:

• Select a source location with nice skin texture.

• To conceal an imperfection, use the Healing Brush with Photoshop's sampled texture.

3. Clone Stamp Tool:

• Ideal for removing major defects or exact copying of things.

How it works:

• Select a source region by holding Alt (Windows) or Option (Mac) and clicking.

• To clone an imperfection, paint over the original area to create a flaw.

4. Patch Tool:

• For removing bigger defects or objects, choose and move a piece of healthy skin to cover the problem.

Tips to Remove Blemishes:

• Zoom in for fine picture editing.

• To get a natural effect, use a soft brush with a size slightly bigger than the imperfection and modify the hardness.

• Create a new layer atop the background layer to quickly undo and change modifications.

• Subtle retouching is key to creating a natural-looking photograph.

Photoshop tools for erasing blemishes: Spot Healing Brush, Healing Brush, Clone Stamp, and Patch Tool.

By learning these tools and methods, you can efficiently erase flaws and faults from your photographs, yielding more polished and professional-looking results.

Adjusting the Brightness and Contrast in Photoshop

• Controls the brightness of a picture.

• Increasing brightness makes the picture lighter.

• **Decreased brightness**: Darkens the picture.

• **Contrast**: Adjusts the disparity between bright and dark regions of a picture.

• Increasing contrast brightens the highlights and darkens the shadows.

• Decreased contrast creates a flat and washed-out appearance.

Methods to Adjust Brightness and Contrast:

1.Brightness/contrast Adjustment Layer:

• To create a new adjustment layer, go to Layer > New Adjustment Layer > Brightness/Contrast.

• Use the sliders to adjust the brightness and contrast.

• Non-Destructive: This approach produces a new layer for the alteration, making it easy to change or delete the effect afterward.

2.Image > Adjustments > Brightness and Contrast:

• **Direct Adjustment:** This method alters the image's brightness and contrast.

• **Limited flexibility**: Changes are applied directly to image data, making them difficult to reverse or modify later.

3.Curve Adjustment Layer:

• **More Control:** Create custom curves for precise brightness and contrast control.

• **Increased flexibility**: Offers more precise adjustments compared to the basic Brightness/Contrast sliders.

Tips for adjusting the brightness and contrast:

• **Use the Histogram**: The histogram in the Adjustments panel provides a visual representation of the image's tonal distribution. Use it as a guideline to make informed changes.

• Begin with subtle tweaks and progressively increase the impact to get the desired appearance.

• Always use an adjustment layer for non-destructive editing.

Photoshop Brightness/Contrast Adjustment Layer.

Understanding how to modify brightness and contrast allows you to substantially increase the visual impact of your photographs, making them look more colorful, lively, and visually attractive.

Color Correction and Grading in Photoshop

Color correction and grading are important strategies for improving the visual appeal and mood of your photographs. While they may seem identical, there are several major differences:

Color Correction:

• **Focus**: Primarily on attaining correct color representation.

- **Goals**:

- **Correcting white balance**: Ensuring that white objects appear white in the image.

- **Fixing color casts:** Removing undesired color tints (e.g., a blue or orange cast).

- **Adjusting exposure**: Ensuring optimum brightness and contrast.

- **Techniques:**

To modify white balance, use the White Balance tool or the Properties panel's Temperature and Tint settings.

- **Levels and Curves**: Adjusting the tone range of the picture.

- **Hue/Saturation**: Changing the hue, saturation, and luminance of certain colors or ranges.

Color Grading:

- Focus on creating a certain atmosphere or creative style.

- **Goals**:

- Enhance mood by creating a warm, cold, or dramatic appearance.

- To create a distinct look, use stylistic color filters and effects.

- **Matching a desired look**: Replicating a film's color palette or visual style.

Techniques:

49

- **Color Lookup**: Use Look Up Tables (LUTs) to immediately change an image's color.

- Creating bespoke curves for each color channel (RGB, Red, Green, Blue) to enhance color accuracy.

- Selective color adjusts certain color ranges within a picture.

- Gradient Maps provide gradual color shifts over a picture.

Tools for color correction and grading in Photoshop:

• **Adjustment layers:**

• Curves provide fine control over tone range and hue.

• **Levels**: Adjusts the image's tone range.

• Adjust hue, saturation, and brightness of colors.

• **Color Balance**: Adjusts the image's overall color balance.

Selective Color: Changes the color of selected color ranges.

• Photo Filter simulates the effect of colored filters on the lens.

• Color Lookup uses LUTs to change an image's color.

Tips for Successful Color Correction and Grading:

• Use adjustment layers to retain original picture data and avoid destructive editing.

• Start with simple tweaks and progressively polish the appearance.

• Use reference photos as inspiration or to fit a certain style.

• Experiment with various approaches and settings.

Mastering color correction and grading methods allows you to modify your photographs, increase their visual impact, and achieve spectacular and distinctive outcomes.

Sharpening and smoothing images using Photoshop

Sharpening and smoothing are important methods for improving the visual quality of your photos.

Sharpening

• **Purpose**: Enhances picture sharpness and clarity, including edges and details.

• Use when photographs seem hazy or lack clarity, particularly after resizing or zooming in.

Tools:

• Unsharp Mask is a typical sharpening filter with parameters for Amount, Radius, and Threshold.

• Smart Sharpen is a more sophisticated filter that provides greater control over sharpening, including noise reduction and area-specific sharpening.

• The High Pass Filter emphasizes edges, creating a mild sharpening effect.

Smoothing

• **Purpose**: Reduces noise, softens skin, and improves overall attractiveness.

• **When to use**: To reduce noise in pictures or soften skin tones in portraiture.

• **Tools**:

• The Gaussian Blur filter weakens the whole picture.

• **Surface Blur**: Improves skin texture, decreases noise, and preserves edges.

• **Reduce Noise:** A tool for reducing picture noise.

Tips for Sharpening and Smoothing:

• Use with caution since over-sharpening might cause anomalies such as halos or noise. Over-smoothing may make images seem fuzzy or strange.

• Apply non-destructive sharpening and smoothing effects using adjustment layers or Smart Filters.

• To properly analyze sharpening and smoothing outcomes, zoom in to 100% or greater.

• Experiment with various settings and approaches to get the best effects for your photograph.

Mastering sharpening and smoothing methods allows you to greatly improve the visual quality of your photographs, making them look more crisp, defined, and polished.

Chapter 6

Working with Text

Creating and formatting text layers in Photoshop

Creating text layers

1. Select the Type Tool (T) from the Tools menu.

2. **Click to create text:**

• To generate a single line of text, point to the canvas and click once.

• To create a text box with many lines, click and drag the paragraph content.

3. **Type Your Text**: Begin typing the appropriate text.

Formatting Text

• The Character Panel (Window > Character) offers numerous formatting possibilities.

• Choose a font family (Arial, Times New Roman) and style (bold, italic).

• Adjust the font size.

• **Color**: Select the text color.

• **Kerning**: Adjust character spacing.

• **Tracking**: Adjust character spacing across the text.

• Adjust the spacing between lines of text.

Additional formatting options:

• Use Warp Text to distort text with different styles (e.g., Arc, Flag, Inflate).

• Use layer styles like as drop shadows, glows, and bevels to improve the look of your text.

• Use Warp Text to distort text with different styles (e.g., Arc, Flag, Inflate).

Tips for working with text layers:

• For greater control and editing, create distinct text layers for each line or piece.

• Experiment with Layer Styles to create distinctive and eye-catching text effects.

• To apply filters or effects that are incompatible with text layers, rasterize the text (Layer > Rasterize > Type). This transforms the text to pixels, making it editable just like any other picture layer.

Mastering these methods will allow you to successfully add and format text in your Photoshop projects, resulting in visually attractive designs, headlines, and more.

Text Effects and Styles in Photoshop

Text effects and styles enable you to convert simple text into visually appealing and eye-catching pieces. Photoshop has a variety of choices for enhancing the look of your text, ranging from subtle glows to stunning 3D effects.

Key Methods of Creating Text Effects:

1.Layer styles:

To access the Layer Style dialog box, just double-click the text layer in the Layers panel.

- **Effects**:

- **Drop Shadow**: Creates a shadow from the text.

- **Inner Shadow:** Adds a shadow to the text itself.

- **Outer Glow:** Adds a glowing effect to the text's edges.

- **Inner Glow**: Adds a glowing effect to the text.

- **Bevel and Emboss:** Create a 3D effect for text.

- **Satin**: Creates a light gloss on the text.

- **Color Overlay**: Adds a solid color or gradient to text.

- **Gradient Overlay**: Adds a gradient to the text, creating unique color transitions.

- **Pattern Overlay**: Add a pattern to the text.

- **Stroke**: Creates an outline around the text.

2.**Filters**:

• Gaussian Blur softens text edges, creating a gentle glow effect.

• Motion Blur simulates motion by blurring text in a certain direction.

• To distort text, use filters such as Wave, Ripple, and Shear.

3.**Blending modes:**

Experiment with various blending modes (e.g., Multiply, Screen, Overlay) to alter how the text interacts with the backdrop or layers.

Tips for creating effective text effects:

• Begin with minor effects and progressively raise the intensity.

• Experiment with layer styles and filters to create unique effects.

• Use Layer Masks for fine control over effects.

• **Save Layer Styles**: Preset your preferred text effects for simple use in future projects.

Mastering text effects and styles allows you to boost your designs and produce visually appealing typography.

Working with Type Tools in Photoshop.

Photoshop has a number of tools for producing and modifying text, enabling you to include striking typography into your projects. Here's an overview of major concepts:

1. **Selecting the Type Tool.**

• Locate Type Tool (T) in the Tools panel. It's often associated with other drawing tools.

 Variation:

• The Horizontal Type Tool generates horizontal lines of text.

- The Vertical Type Tool generates vertically oriented text.

- The Horizontal Type Mask Tool makes a selection depending on the shape of the text.

- The Vertical Type Mask Tool makes a vertical selection depending on the shape of the text.

2. Creating Text

- To produce a single line of text, use the Type Tool by clicking once on the canvas.

- Create a text box with many lines by clicking and dragging on the canvas.

3. Editing Text

- To use the Direct Selection Tool, pick the white arrow after creating text.

- To edit individual characters, select and move individual letters or groups of letters.

- To modify the shape of text pathways, use the Horizontal or Vertical Type Mask Tool.

4. Formatting Text

- The Character Panel (Window > Character) allows you to control:

- Select the font family, size, and style (bold, italic, etc.).

- **Color**: Select the text color.

- **Kerning**: Adjust character spacing.

- **Tracking**: Adjust character spacing across the text.

- Adjust the spacing between lines of text.

5. Text Effects

- Use layer styles (drop shadow, glow, bevel) to improve the look of your text.

- **Warp Text:** Use Arc, Flag, or Inflate styles to distort text.

Tips for Working with Type

- For greater control and editing, create distinct text layers for each line or piece.

- Experiment with Layer Styles to create distinctive and eye-catching text effects.

- To apply filters or effects that are incompatible with text layers, rasterize the text (Layer > Rasterize > Type). This transforms the text to pixels, making it editable just like any other picture layer.

Understanding these ideas allows you to efficiently utilize Photoshop's Type Tools to produce professional-looking typography for your projects.

Chapter 7

Filters and Effects

Applying filters in Photoshop

Filters are powerful Photoshop tools that may radically change the look of your photographs. They may be used for creative effects, picture upgrades, or even to fix flaws.

Accessing Filters:

• Open the "Filter" option at the top of the Photoshop interface. There are several filter categories available, including blur, sharpen, stylize, artistic, and more.

• To access many filters in one location, go to Filter > Filter Gallery.

Applying filters:

1. Choose the layer on which you wish to apply the filter.

2. Select the appropriate filter from either the Filter menu or the Filter Gallery.

3. Most filters have changeable settings. Experiment with the parameters to get the desired result.

4. **Preview (optional):** The Filter Gallery enables you to see the filter effect before applying it.

5. Click the "OK" button to apply the filter to your picture.

Types of Filters:

• **Blur:**

• Gaussian Blur softens the picture uniformly.

• Motion Blur simulates motion by blurring images in a certain direction.

• **Surface Blur:** Improves skin tones and minimizes noise while maintaining edges.

• **Sharpen**:

• Unsharp Mask improves edge sharpness and clarity.

• **Smart Sharpen**: Improves sharpening control and reduces noise levels.

• **Stylize**:

• **Embellish**: Creates a 3D effect.

• **Find Edges**: Identifies and highlights image edges.

• Solarize inverts the image's tones.

• **Artistic**:

• **Poster Edges:** Achieves a posterized look with strong edges.

• **Plastic Wrap:** Creates the look of plastic wrap on the picture.

• **Distortion:**

• **Twirl**: Moves the picture around a central point.

• Shear skews a picture horizontally or vertically.

Tips for Using Filters

• Enable non-destructive editing by applying filters as Smart Filters (Layer > Smart Objects > Convert to Smart Object).

• Experiment with filters and settings to uncover unique effects.

• Combine filters and layer masks to apply effects to particular sections of a picture.

By experimenting with the many filters available in Photoshop, you may unleash your creativity and modify your photographs in limitless ways.

Exploring Creative Filters (e.g., Liquify, Vanish)

You're correct to concentrate on some of the more imaginative and distinctive filters! Let's go into two of them:

1. Liquify

• The Liquify filter warps and distorts visuals. Consider it digital clay; you can push, pull, bloat, and pucker pixels to sculpt features, create creative effects, and even slightly edit photographs.

Key tools:

• **Forward Warp Tool**: Move pixels in any direction.

• The Pucker Tool pulls pixels towards the center of the brush.

• The Bloat Tool pushes pixels away from the center of the brush.

- The Reconstruct Tool smooths out distortions and recovers sections that have been overly deformed.

- **Creative Applications:**

- Use artistic effects to create weird and abstract pictures.

- Refine portrait features such as eyes, noses, and lips.

- To create a cartoonish or stylized style, exaggerate character traits.

2. Vanish

The Vanish tool, a recent addition to Photoshop, removes undesirable elements from photos. It employs AI to effectively evaluate the surrounding environment and seamlessly replace the deleted item.

- **How it works:**

- To delete an item, first pick it using any available selection tool.

- To apply Vanish, go to Edit > Fill > Vanish.

- Adjust options to control the fill intensity and algorithm's alignment with the surrounding region.

Key uses:

- Remove distracting items from photographs, such as power wires and people.

- Retouching involves removing flaws and small defects.

- Create creative compositions by removing components from images.

Tips for Applying Creative Filters:

• Convert your layer to a Smart Object before using Liquify to retain the original picture data.

• Create a History State before making significant changes using Liquify to quickly reverse them.

• Experiment to create astonishing effects.

By studying these creative filters and playing with their settings, you may open up a world of artistic possibilities and change your photographs in unexpected ways.

Using adjustment layers as filters

Adjustment layers are a powerful and non-destructive tool for creating "filter-like" effects in Photoshop. Here's how they function and why they're so useful:

What are the Adjustment Layers?

• They live on a distinct layer above your picture data.

• **Non-Destructive:** They do not affect the original pixel information of your picture. This enables you to quickly alter or remove the effect later without damaging the original picture.

• **Flexibility**: Easily modify effect strength, apply layer masks, and alter blending mode for creative effects.

Common Adjustment Layers Used as Filter:

• Use custom curves to precisely modify brightness, contrast, and color.

• **Levels**: Adjust the image's tonal range, similar to Curves.

• Control the hue, saturation, and brightness of colors in images.

• Adjust the color balance of the picture.

• The Photo Filter simulates the impact of colored filters on the lens.

• **Gradient Map**: Add a gradient overlay to the picture to create a stunning tone change.

• Convert picture to black and white with configurable tonal settings.

• **Example: Applying a Gradient Map as a Filter**

1.To create a Gradient Map Adjustment Layer, go to Layer > New Adjustment Layer > Gradient Map.

2.Choose a Gradient: From the list of possibilities, choose a gradient (for example, black to white or black to color).

3.Adjust the Gradient: Change the gradient by adding or subtracting color stops.

4.Change the Blending Mode: Experiment with various blending modes (for example, Overlay, Soft Light, and Multiply) to observe how the gradient interacts with the picture.

Key Advantages:

• Non-Destructive Workflow: Adjust or eliminate the effect at any moment.

• Use layer masks to control the effect's strength and application.

• Use many adjustment layers to create complex and distinctive effects.

Using adjustment layers as filters gives you greater control and flexibility in your picture editing process. You may try out various effects, fine-tune the results, and quickly add or delete them as required.

Chapter 8

Digital Painting and Drawing

The Brush Tool is one of Photoshop's most essential tools. It enables you to paint directly on your picture or canvas, much like a real brush. Here's the breakdown:

1. Selecting and Using the Brush Tool

• Find the Brush Tool (B) in the Tools panel.

• **Paintings**:

• To create paint strokes, just click and drag your mouse over the canvas.

• To adjust the brush size, use the bracket keys [and] or the Size slider in the Options bar.

• Control the softness or hardness of the brush's edges. A harsh brush provides sharp edges, while a soft brush produces softer, more blended strokes.

2. Brush Tip Shapes

• Photoshop provides a diverse range of brush tip shapes, from simple circles and squares to complex patterns and textures.

• Use the Brush Picker in the Options tab to switch between various brush tips.

• Create and store custom brush tips.

3. Brush dynamics

• **Control**: Use the Brush Dynamics section in the Options bar to adjust the brush's response to pen pressure, tilt, and other parameters (for pressure-sensitive styluses).

• **Options are:**

• Vary the size of brush strokes to create jitter.

• Vary the opacity of brush strokes to get jitter effect.

• **Angle Jitter**: Adjust the angle of brush strokes.

• **Roundness Jitter**: Adjust brush tip roundness.

4. **Common Uses**

• Design digital artwork, illustrations, and paintings.

• Retouching includes removing imperfections, retouching skin, and repairing photos.

• To create layer masks, paint with black and white.

• Create distinctive effects, such as texture or abstract patterns.

Tips for Using the Brush Tool

• Experiment with various brush tips, sizes, and settings to see what affects you can produce.

• Recommend using a pressure-sensitive tablet for better control and a more natural painting experience.

• Save your preferred brush settings as custom brushes for easy access in future projects.

Mastering the Brush Tool and its numerous options will allow you to paint, sketch, and edit photos in Photoshop with more accuracy and creativity.

Creating custom brushes in Photoshop

Creating custom brushes helps you to broaden your creative toolset and generate distinctive painting results. Here's a step-by-step instruction:

1. **Prepare your source image**.

• Create a new, transparent document in Photoshop.

• **Draw or import**:

• Use the Pen Tool, Brush Tool, or other drawing tools to create the desired brush form or pattern.

• Import a picture (e.g., texture, leaf, splattered paint effect) to use as the brush tip.

• **Prepare the image.**

• To clean up your source image's edges, use the Eraser Tool or other tools as needed.

• Adjust contrast to clearly define the shape against the backdrop.

2. **Define the Brush**

• To utilize a form or picture as a brush tip, first choose the source.

• To define a brush preset, go to Edit > Define Brush Preset.

• Name your brush: Give it a descriptive name.

• Click OK to add your new custom brush to the Brush Preset Picker.

3. **Customize your brush (optional).**

• Customize your brush's behavior in the Brush Settings window after creating it.

• **Shape Dynamics**: Adjust the size, angle, and roundness of the brush tip based on pen pressure and other parameters.

• Scatter brush strokes to create a more textured impression.

• **Texture**: Apply texture to brush strokes.

Tips for Making Effective Custom Brushes

• Begin with basic shapes or graphics to get experience with the technique.

• Experiment with various brush settings to see how they impact the look of your strokes.

• Organize and store bespoke brushes for convenient access in future projects.

Create and use custom brushes to add unique textures, patterns, and creative effects to your digital artwork.

Digital Painting Techniques in Photoshop

Photoshop's digital painting feature provides a huge canvas for creativity. Here are a few crucial approaches to consider:

1. **Layering**:

• Begin with a basic color layer then add additional layers for shadows, highlights, and details.

• Experiment with blending modes (Multiply, Overlay, Screen) between layers to create unique effects.

• Use layer masks to control the opacity of certain sections of a layer, enabling precise blending and refining.

2. **Brushwork**:

• Use various brush types (hard, soft, textured) to replicate different painting media (e.g., oil paints, watercolors, charcoal).

• To produce dynamic and expressive strokes, adjust brush properties such as size, opacity, and angle jitter.

• Adjust brush opacity for smooth transitions and delicate mixes.

3. **Color Theory:**

• Create harmonious color palettes using color wheels, pickers, and libraries.

• Consider color value (lightness/darkness) to enhance depth and dimension.

• Use cool and warm hues to create the tone and setting.

4. **Rendering Techniques:**

• **Blocking in**: Begin with big shapes and progressively refine details.

• When layering colors, start with lighter washes and progressively add deeper layers for depth and shadows.

• Use the Smudge Tool and other blending tools to soften edges and create seamless transitions.

5. Studying Masters:

• Analyze great artists' approaches to learn about composition, color theory, and brushwork.

• Use online tutorials, seminars, and artist groups to get inspiration and advice.

6. Practice and experimentation:

• Regular practice is essential for enhancing your digital painting abilities.

• Experiment with various approaches, brush settings, and color combinations.

By understanding these skills and regularly practicing, you may unleash your creativity and produce magnificent digital artworks in Photoshop.

Chapter 9

Photomontage and Compositing

Adding Multiple Images in Photoshop

Combining numerous pictures in Photoshop is an effective approach for generating photomontages, surreal compositions, and other effects. Here's a breakdown of the procedure:

1. **Open and arrange images.**

• Open photos to mix in Photoshop.

• Create a new document with adequate dimensions to fit all photographs.

• To add images to a new document, drag & drop them from their own windows. This generates distinct layers for each picture in the Layers window.

2. **Position and Resize.**

• Use the Move Tool (V) to place images in the new document.

• Use Free Transform (Ctrl+T/Cmd+T) to resize, rotate, and scale images as required.

3. **Blend Images**

• Experiment with layer blending modes (e.g., Multiply, Screen, Overlay) to create unique picture combinations.

• Adjust layer opacity to regulate visibility and interaction with other pictures.

• Use layer masks to selectively show or conceal picture elements, resulting in seamless transitions and realistic blends.

4. Refine and enhance

• Use the Refine Edge tool to create a smoother picture merge.

• Use adjustment layers (e.g., Curves, Levels, Color Balance) to fine-tune color and tone in the composite picture.

• Enhance the composition with finishing touches like shadows, highlights, and other elements for a more realistic and visually appealing look.

Tips for combining images:

• Select photographs with appropriate lighting, perspective, and style.

• Before integrating photographs, plan your composition and consider how the pieces will interact.

• Use adjustment layers and layer masks for non-destructive editing and quick modifications.

• Experiment with various methods and picture pairings to create your distinctive style.

Mastering these methods allows you to create amazing and inventive compositions by smoothly merging various pictures in Photoshop.

Creating realistic compositions.

To create realistic composites in Photoshop, you must pay close attention to detail and have a good sense of visual harmony. Here are some important techniques:

1. Lighting and shadows

• **Match Lighting Conditions:** Select photographs with comparable lighting (e.g., taken outside on a sunny day or in a studio with constant lighting).

• Use adjustment layers (Curves, Levels) to match the foreground element's shadows and highlights to the backdrop.

• To create realistic shadows, use the Drop Shadow layer style or manually paint them on the foreground element in the scene.

2. Perspective and depth:

• **Match Perspective**: Ensure the foreground element's perspective matches the backdrop. Adjust the perspective of the foreground element using the Transform tools (Scale, Rotate, and Perspective).

• To generate depth in a composition, blur distant parts, modify atmospheric perspective, and use a shallow depth of focus.

3. Color and tone:

• **Color Matching**: Use adjustment layers (Color Balance, Hue/Saturation) to match foreground and background colors.

• **Create Color Harmony:** Coordinate colors to produce a visually pleasing and harmonious arrangement.

4. Refine edges:

• Use the Refine Edge Tool to create a smooth blend between the foreground and background.

• Use the Refine Edge tool's Decontaminate Colors option to eliminate color fringing from edges.

5. Subtlety is key

• Resist the impulse to over-edit images. Subtle modifications are often more successful in producing a realistic and convincing composite.

• **Step back and evaluate**: Take pauses from editing to get a new perspective and find places for improvement.

Example: Composing a Person into a New Scene

1.**Finding Suitable Images:** Choose a high-quality photograph of a person and a backdrop image that compliments the topic.

2.**Isolate the Subject**: Using selection and refine edge tools, carefully clip out the subject from their original surroundings.

3.**Match Lighting and Perspective**: Make the subject's lighting and perspective match the backdrop scene.

4.**Blend the topic**: Using layer masks and blending modes, flawlessly blend the topic into the backdrop.

5.**Refine Details**: Use subtle shadows, highlights, and reflections to increase the composition's authenticity.

By carefully examining these aspects and using these strategies, you may create gorgeous and convincing photomontages that smoothly integrate many pictures into a unified and realistic scenario.

Masking and Blending Techniques for Photoshop

Masking and blending are essential for smoothly integrating pictures and creating realistic compositions. Here's a deeper dive.

1. **Layer Masks: The Foundation.**

• A layer mask is a grayscale picture that affects the visibility of the layer it's associated with.

• Black hides the layer's related region.

• White indicates the layer's related region.

• Gray creates varied degrees of transparency.

• **Create a Layer Mask:**

To add a layer mask, click the "Add Layer Mask" button at the bottom of the Layers panel, which resembles a rectangle with a circle within.

To expose an area, first make a selection around it and then click the "Add Layer Mask" button.

• **Editing a layer mask:**

To show or conceal portions of the mask, use the Brush Tool with black and white paint.

Use the Gradient Tool to create seamless transitions between visible and invisible regions.

2. Blending modes

• Blending modes control how a layer's colors interact with those below.

• Key blending modes for compositing.

• **Multiply**: Darkens colors that overlap. Ideal for deepening shadows.

• **Screen**: Lightens colors that overlap.

• **Overlay**: Achieves a balance between multiply and screen.

• **Soft Light**: Colors are subtly lightened or darkened, akin to a soft light.

• Hard light is more dramatic than soft light, resulting in greater contrast.

3. Refining edges

• Use the Refine Edge Tool to enhance a selection's natural mix.

• **Smooth**: Reduces jagged edges.

• **Feather**: Softens edges of selection.

• **Contrast**: Adjust the contrast between the topic and backdrop.

• **Radius**: Adjusts the breadth of the edge refining area.

- **Decontaminate Colors**: Removes color fringing from borders.

4. Combining Techniques

• Use layer masks to regulate where a blending mode is applied.

• **Adjustment Layers with Masks**: Use layer masks to govern the regions where adjustments are made, such as curves, levels, and color balance.

Key Takeaways

• Successful picture compositing requires a strong understanding of layer masks and blending modes.

Why Experimentation is crucial! To get the desired results, experiment with various method combinations.

• Use the Refine Edge tool to seamlessly combine pictures.

You may use these strategies to create amazing and lifelike compositions in Photoshop.

Chapter 10

Working with Paths

Creating and editing paths in Photoshop

Paths are vector-based outlines that may be created and edited in Photoshop. They are very adaptable and have several applications, ranging from making exact choices to sketching complicated forms.

1. Creating paths

• The Pen Tool (P) is the main tool for generating routes.

• Click to construct anchor points that define the path's corners and bends.

• Create curved segments by clicking and dragging between anchor points.

• To draw straight lines between anchor points, just click and release.

• Hold Shift and click to confine lines to 45-degree angles.

• Rectangle, Ellipse, and other shape tools may be used to design routes.

2. Editing Paths

• **Use Direct Selection Tool (A).**

• To change the geometry of the route, select and move individual anchor points.

• Adjust the direction handles to alter the curvature of route segments.

• To use the Convert Point Tool, press Shift+C.

• Convert Corner Points to Smooth Points: Create smooth curves connecting anchor points.

• Convert smooth points to sharp corners along the route.

3. **Using Paths**

• **Create selections.**

• To use the route Selection Tool (A), choose a route from the Paths panel and click the "Make Selection" button in the options bar.

• Use the Refine Edge tool to further refine the route selection.

• **Stroke path:**

• Apply brush strokes along the route.

• Stroke the route with a pencil.

• Fill route with color or pattern.

• Create text in the form of a route.

Tips for Working With Paths

• Zoom in for exact path modification.

• The routes Panel (Window > Paths) shows all current routes and enables for easy selection, renaming, and deletion.

• Consistent practice is essential for learning route building and modification procedures.

Understanding how to generate and modify paths gives you more control over your artwork and opens up new creative possibilities in Photoshop.

Using Paths for Selection and Shapes

1. Creating selections from paths

• To pick a route, use the route Selection Tool (A) in the Tools panel after generating it.

• Click the "Make Selection" button in the Options box.

• Use the Refine Edge tool to fine-tune the path-based selection.

• Add feathering to the choices for a delicate edge.

2. **Creating Shapes from Paths**.

• **Fill the path:**

• Select the route from the Paths window.

• To fill the path, pick a color or pattern from Edit > Fill Path menu.

• **Stroke path:**

• Select the route from the Paths window.

• To stroke a path, pick Edit > Stroke Path and a brush or pencil tool.

3. **Using Paths as Clipping Mask**

- To create a clipping mask, draw a path around the desired region.

- To cut a layer, create a new layer above it.

- In the Paths panel, choose the "Make Work Path" button.

- To create a clipping mask, right-click on the new layer and pick "Create Clipping Mask." This will clip the layer's content to the path shape.

4. **Working with vector shapes.**

- Use shape tools such as Rectangle, Ellipse, and Polygon to construct vector forms.

- Edit the form's path using the Direct Selection Tool to change its size, shape, and location.

- Convert the shape to a shape layer for layer styles, effects, and modifications.

Key Benefits of Using Paths

- Create precise and sophisticated choices.

- Easy to alter and change shapes and choices.

- **Non-destructive**: Shapes and selections may be made without permanently affecting the picture pixels.

- Paths are versatile and may be used to create unique shapes or isolate parts in a picture.

Mastering the procedures for constructing and manipulating paths will provide you with a strong tool for precision selection, form construction, and image modification in Photoshop.

Chapter 11

Actions and Batch Processing

Creating and Running Actions in Photoshop

Photoshop Actions are an effective approach to automate repetitive operations, saving you valuable time and effort. Here's how to build and operate them:

1. Creating an Action

• To access the Actions Panel, go to Window > Actions.

• Create a new action.

• Click the "Create New Action" button at the bottom of the Actions window.

• Give your action a name and attach it to a set.

• Click "Record."

• Automate desired actions (e.g., modifications, filters, resizing).

• Stop recording by clicking the "Stop" button in the Actions menu.

2. Running an action

• Select the desired action from the Actions panel.

• Play the Action:

• Click the "Play" button at the bottom of the Actions window.

• Alternatively, use the keyboard shortcut associated to the action.

3. Editing an Action.

• To open the action, double-click on it in the Actions panel.

• **Editing Steps**:

• Add, remove, or edit specific stages in the action.

• Adjust parameters per step.

• To save changes, click the "Done" button after editing an action.

4. Batch Processing

• Automate tasks on many pictures using File > Automate > Batch.

Tips For Creating Effective Actions:

• **Keep it basic:** Begin with simple activities and progressively add complexity.

• Use keyboard shortcuts to speed up your activities.

• Conduct thorough testing on several photos to confirm desired results.

• Organize your activities by creating sets and folders for simple access.

Examples of useful actions:

• **Photo Processing Workflow**: Steps for adjusting brightness, contrast, and sharpness.

• Batch resize photos to precise proportions.

• **Watermarking**: Add a watermark to several photos.

• **Creative Effects**: Use filters and changes to create a distinct artistic style.

By developing and using Actions, you may dramatically optimize your Photoshop process and save time.

Automating repetitive tasks

• **You're right**: Actions are quite useful for automating repetitive operations in Photoshop. Here's a closer look into batch processing and generating more sophisticated actions:

1. Batch Processing

• Batch processing lets you apply an action to several photos in one step.

How to use:

• Go to File > Automate > Batch to open the Batch processing dialog box.

• Select the Action you wish to apply.

• **Source**:

• Select a folder containing the photographs to process.

• Process pictures from the full disk or folder hierarchy.

• Select a destination for the processed photos.

• Save processed pictures in the same folder as the originals.

- **Folder**: Choose a different location to store processed photographs.

- **No Destination**: After processing, leave images open in Photoshop.

Image Processing Options:

- Select the color mode for the processed pictures (e.g., RGB or Grayscale).

- Select the bit depth for the processed pictures.

- Set the resolution of processed pictures.

- **Error Handling:** Determine how to handle potential errors while processing.

- Click "Run" to start batch processing.

2. **Creating Complex Actions**

- **Conditional steps:**

- Use if/then statements to include conditional phases in your action. For example, you might include a phase that checks the picture size and only applies particular effects if the image is larger than a given size.

- **Loops**:

- Repeat specific steps from an Action many times. This is handy for doing several iterations of a filter or modification.

- **List of variables:**

• Use variables to tailor the Action for various pictures. For example, you may use a variable to change the file name or the strength of an effect depending on picture properties.

Tips to Automate Repetitive Tasks

• Break down difficult activities into smaller, more manageable actions.

• Thoroughly test your actions on a small group of photographs before processing a large number of files.

• Before conducting batch processing, back up your original photos.

• Experiment with various combinations of stages and parameters to build effective and efficient actions.

By understanding these approaches, you may greatly boost your Photoshop efficiency and automate many of your monotonous activities, giving you more time for creative projects.

Chapter 12

3D using Photoshop

Basic 3D concepts in Photoshop

Photoshop provides a fairly comprehensive 3D workspace. While not a specialist 3D modeling software, the application allows you to design, modify, and render basic 3D objects. Here are some basic 3D ideas to understand:

1. 3D Space:

• 3D things have three dimensions (width, height, and depth), unlike 2D pictures.

• The 3D space is defined by its axes (X, Y, and Z).

• X-axis is horizontal (left to right).

• **Y-axis**: Vertical (up/down)

• **Z-axis**: Depth (forward/backward).

2. Three-dimensional objects:

• Primitive 3D forms include cubes, spheres, cylinders, cones, and pyramids.

• **Extruded Objects**: 2D forms, such as text or logos, may be transformed into 3D objects.

• Import 3D models from other apps (.obj files).

3. 3D views:

• **Multiple perspectives**: View a 3D object from various angles (front, rear, top, bottom, left, and right).

• Rotate the camera around a 3D object to observe it from various angles.

• Zoom in/out to change viewing distance.

4. **Lighting**:

• Photoshop offers virtual lights (ambient, spot, and directional) to create shadows and illuminate 3D objects.

• The location and intensity of lighting impact the shadows created by 3D objects.

5. **Materials**:

• Add textures to 3D objects to enhance their realistic look.

• Photoshop offers a range of materials, including metal, plastic, and glass, each with unique reflecting and refractive qualities.

6. **Rendering**:

Photoshop's rendering engine calculates lighting and shading for 3D scenes.

• Adjust rendering options (such as quality and anti-aliasing) to customize the look of the final picture.

Key takeaways:

• Understanding fundamental 3D concepts such as space, objects, lighting, and materials is essential while using Photoshop.

• The 3D workspace offers tools to manipulate objects, modify lighting, and manage the rendering process.

Photoshop provides a decent basis for basic 3D work, however it lacks the feature-richness of specialist modeling applications.

Create and Edit 3D Objects with Photoshop.

Photoshop provides a fairly comprehensive 3D workspace. While not a specialist 3D modeling software, the application allows you to design, modify, and render basic 3D objects. Here are several important aspects:

1. **Creating 3D objects.**

• **From 2D shapes:**

• Extrude 2D forms made using Shape Tools into 3D objects using the Z-axis.

• Select a shape layer.

• Click 3D > New 3D Extrusion from Selected Layer.

• Change the depth and bevel settings in the Properties section.

• **Three-dimensional primitives:**

To construct basic 3D forms, choose New 3D Layer from the 3D menu. Examples include cubes, spheres, cylinders, and cones.

• **Import 3D models:**

• Photoshop allows you to import 3D models from other apps (e.g.,.obj files).

2. Editing 3D Objects

• Use the Move Tool (V) to translate and move 3D objects in space.

• Use the Rotate Tool to rotate an object around the X, Y, and Z axes.

• Use the Scale Tool to resize an item evenly or along particular axes.

• Use 3D manipulators (cube, sphere, and arrow) in the workspace to accurately position and rotate objects.

• **Properties Panel**: View detailed settings for the 3D object, such as:

• Position the item in 3D space.

• **Rotation**: Rotate the item along each axis.

• **Scale**: Change the object's size.

3. Applying Materials

• Add textures to 3D objects using pictures such as wood, metal, or cloth.

• Control the appearance of an item by adjusting its material qualities such as diffuse color, specular highlights, and bump maps.

Tips for Working With 3D in Photoshop

• Begin with simple shapes and progressively add complexity.

• Experiment with lighting, materials, and camera angles to discover new creative possibilities.

• Use the 3D Panel to access tools and options for 3D objects in Photoshop.

By following these methods and experimenting with Photoshop's 3D tools, you may build and incorporate intriguing 3D components into your designs.

Chapter 13

Tips and Tricks for Mastering Photoshop

Optimize Your Photoshop Workflow

A simplified approach may substantially increase your productivity and make Photoshop more pleasant. Here are a few major strategies:

1. **Workspace Optimization**:

• **Customize your workspace**.

• Arrange panels by docking them where you use them most often.

• Create customized workspaces for various jobs, such as photography, painting, and web design.

• **Keyboard shortcuts:**

• Memorize commonly used shortcuts, such as Ctrl/Cmd+S for saving and Ctrl/Cmd+J for duplicating a layer.

• Customize keyboard shortcuts to your liking.

2. **Non-destructive Editing:**

• Use adjustment layers (Curves, Levels, Hue/Saturation) to make non-destructive color and tone alterations.

• Convert layers to Smart Objects to retain picture data and enable non-destructive filter applications.

• Use layer masks to regulate layer visibility without permanently modifying picture data.

3. **Efficient Selection Techniques**:

• Use the Refine Edge tool to make precise and accurate choices.

• Use the AI-powered Select topic tool for fast and easy topic selection.

• Experiment with various selection tools (e.g., marquee, lasso, magic wand) to determine the most effective way for each assignment.

4. **Using Actions and Scripts:**

• Automate repetitive activities using Actions, such as resizing, sharpening, and adding watermarks.

• Automate difficult activities by using web scripts or creating your own.

5. **Hardware and Software Considerations:**

• **Enough RAM:** Ensure your computer can handle massive files and sophisticated procedures.

• A specialized graphics card (GPU) enhances performance, particularly for 3D work and complicated effects.

• Regularly upgrade your operating system, drivers, and Photoshop software to optimize performance and access the newest features.

6. **Practice and Consistency**

- Regular practice is essential for enhancing your workflow.

- Regularly analyze your process to discover opportunities for improvement.

- Improve your Photoshop skills by watching tutorials, reading articles, and learning from others.

By applying these tactics, you may improve your Photoshop workflow, boost your productivity, and devote more time to the creative parts of your job.

Troubleshooting Common Issues with Photoshop

Here's a summary of typical Photoshop difficulties and how to fix them:

1. Performance Issues (Lagging and Slowdowns)

• Insufficient resources.

- Make sure you have adequate RAM (16GB or more is recommended).

- A dedicated graphics card may considerably boost performance.

- Use an SSD for quicker loading and saving.

- Excessive layering or large files:

- Merge compatible layers to minimize total number of layers.

- Flattening a picture eliminates the need to alter individual layers.

• Close background apps that may be using system resources.

• Optimize performance settings.

• Navigate to Edit > Preferences > Performance to alter options such as Scratch Disks, Memory Usage, and GPU options.

• Clear Cache: Select Edit > Purge > All to remove temporary files and caches.

2. Tool or Feature Issues

• Tools are not working:

• To reset tools, right-click on the tool in the toolbar and choose "Reset Tool."

• Restarting Photoshop will frequently fix temporary issues.

• Brushes not performing as expected:

• To reset brush settings, right-click the Brush Tool and choose "Reset Tool."

• Check Brush Dynamics: Make sure the parameters are accurate.

• Filters not applying:

• To use non-destructive filters, ensure the layer is a Smart Object.

Ensure the filter is compatible with the picture mode (e.g., not all filters are accessible for 1-bit images).

3. File-related issues

• File corruption:

• Try saving the file in a different format (e.g., PSD, TIFF) to ensure it can be opened properly.

• If the file is substantially corrupted, it may be necessary to utilize file recovery software (although this is not guaranteed).

• File compatibility:

• **Check file formats**: Use the appropriate format for the intended purpose (e.g., JPEG for online, TIFF for print).

• Ensure the picture is in the appropriate color mode (e.g., RGB for online, CMYK for print).

4. Workspace and Interface Issues

• To restore the default workspace, go to Window > Workspace and choose Reset All Workspaces.

• Reset preferences

• Hold Alt+Ctrl+Shift (Windows) or Option+Cmd+Shift (Mac) upon startup.

• Select "Yes" to erase the preference file.

• Update graphics drivers to the latest version.

5. General Troubleshooting

• Restart Photoshop to remedy minor bugs and performance concerns.

• Restart your computer to repair system-wide problems that may impair Photoshop.

If you discover a particular problem, share further information (e.g., error messages, specific symptoms) to enable more focused troubleshooting.